W9-CDS-269

KILLER WHALES

Dorothy Hinshaw Patent

photographs by
John K.B. Ford

Holiday House/New York

Library of Congress Cataloging-in-Publication Data
Patent, Dorothy Hinshaw.
Killer whales / Dorothy Hinshaw Patent ; photos. by John K. B. Ford.
p.   cm.
Summary: Describes the physical characteristics, behavior, and
habitats of killer whales.
ISBN 0-8234-0999-6
1. Killer whale—Juvenile literature.   [1. Killer whale.
2. Whales.]   I. Ford, John K. B., ill.   II. Title.
QL737.C432P382   1993   92–23949   CIP   AC
599.5′3–dc20

Thanks to Graeme Ellis for the photograph on page 16.

For all those who work towards human understanding and respect for other species.

D.H.P.

Killer whales are beautiful. Their bodies are covered with bright patches of black and white. They are more closely related to dolphins than they are to other whales such as humpbacks. Like whales and dolphins, killer whales are mammals. That means they breathe air and feed their young with milk.

A killer whale breaches, throwing its huge body completely out of the water.

Two killer whales blow out air, producing clouds of moisture above their heads.

Each whale has a blowhole on the top of its head for breathing. As the animal swims, it brings the front of its body out of the water and blows air out of the blowhole with a loud *whoosh*. Then it takes in a new breath. Before it goes under again, the whale closes the blowhole to keep out water. Normally, the animal stays underwater from one to four minutes between breaths. But it can stay down for as long as twenty minutes.

Surrounded by droplets from its blow, a killer whale takes air into its blowhole.

You can see the smooth hairless skin on this young killer whale.

Like other mammals, killer whales always keep their bodies at the same warm temperature. But unlike land mammals and seals, killer whales do not have fur to hold in the warmth. Instead, a thick layer of fat under the skin, called blubber, helps keep their bodies warm.

Whales have four fins. The top one is called the "dorsal fin."

Instead of legs or arms, whales have one pair of fins called flippers at the sides of their bodies. The flippers help steer the animal through the water.

A killer whale lies on its side, showing one of its flippers.

Their tails are made up of a fin with two halves, called "flukes." When the whale swims, the flukes move up and down. Killer whales are powerful swimmers. They can go as fast as 28 miles an hour.

A killer whale slaps its flukes on the water's surface.

You can see the eye of this whale in the dark area in the center of the photo.

The eyes of whales can see well under water. They can also see in the air. Killer whales sometimes poke their heads out of the water to look around. This is called "spy hopping."

A killer whale spy hopping. To the right is the dorsal fin of another whale.

The ears of whales are inside their heads. All you can see on the outside is a small hole. Sound carries far in the water. Killer whales use sound to help find their way around and to locate their prey. They send out a rapid series of clicks and listen for the echoes that bounce back. The echoes tell the whale what lies ahead.

Killer whales are big. A male can grow as long as 32 feet. His dorsal fin can reach a height of 5½ feet, taller than an average woman. He can weigh up to 9 tons, as much as 140 persons put together.

Females are smaller. They can reach 28 feet in length and weigh as much as 4.5 tons. Their dorsal fins are about three feet high.

A five-day-old calf nurses.

At birth, a killer whale is already seven feet long and weighs 300 pounds. It is born fifteen to sixteen months after its mother mates. Normally, the female has one baby at a time. The baby, called a calf, depends completely on its mother for food and protection. It drinks rich milk from its mother's teats. The teats are tucked away inside slits on her belly.

A female killer whale begins to have young when she is about 14 years old. From then on, she gives birth every four to six years. She stops having calves when she is around 40 years of age. She may live, however, up to 75 years.

The mother and her calf stay close together.

A male killer whale with a tall dorsal fin.

Scientists are not sure when male killer males begin to
breed. The dorsal fin of a male killer whale begins to
grow when he is about 14 years old. The male whales
keep growing until they are around twenty.

Killer whales have rows of bright white teeth. They line both the top and bottom jaws. The teeth curve slightly backward. Each whale has from 40 to 56 teeth. The biggest ones are about 2 inches long. The teeth are used in hunting and feeding.

Scientists call the killer whale *Orcinus orca*. They are named killer whales because they are powerful hunters. Some people prefer to use the name "orca." When scientists study killer whales, they photograph the dorsal fin of each one and the gray "saddle patch" behind it. The fin and patch look different on each animal. This allows the scientists to tell the whales apart.

Scientists photographing killer whales. You can see that both the fins and the saddle patches of these two animals look very different.

A transient pod.

Scientists in southern British Columbia, Canada, have been studying killer whales for years. They have learned many things about these intelligent animals. Each year they learn more.

Killer whales live in family groups called "pods." The British Columbian scientists now know there are two different kinds of pods. "Transient" (TRANZ-ee-ent) pods travel long distances. They are small groups of usually no more than five individuals. Transient killer whales feed mostly on marine mammals like seals and porpoises.

Resident pods usually have 10 to 20 animals. After studying the whales over a period of years, scientists discovered that the whales in one pod are related. Both male and female killer whales stay with their mothers after they grow up. Each pod is really a family—related females, their offspring, and their daughters' offspring. So far, scientists haven't figured out which whales the fathers are.

A female whale (in front) rests with two of her sons.

When a pod gets too big, it may split up into two smaller pods. This happens gradually. One female and her offspring may begin to spend some of their time away from the rest of the pod. As time goes by, they spend more and more of their time away. But related pods come together to visit, just like human families do. The whales play, rubbing together, nibbling each other, and chasing and leaping.

Killer whales playing together.

Killer whales use sounds to "talk" to each other. These whistles and other sounds are different from the clicks they use in hunting. When pod members are separated, they keep in touch by making sounds.

Scientists use underwater microphones to study killer whale sounds. Transient pods are quieter than residents. Scientists have a hard time recording sounds from them.

Each resident pod has a basic set of about ten sounds. The animals learn them from their families as they grow up.

By studying the differences in the sounds made by the pods in southwestern Canada, scientists have figured out how the various pods are related. The sounds used by a family change slowly over time. For this reason, if pods have been separated from one another for a long period, their sounds become different.

When pod members are busy feeding, they can become separated (notice the one whale way behind the others). But they can keep in touch through the sounds they make.

Killer whales live in all the world's oceans. They prefer cool waters along coastlines. Sometimes they even swim up into river mouths. But they have been seen as far as a thousand miles from land.

There are many captive killer whales at parks and aquariums. Scientists have learned a lot about these intelligent animals by studying the captives. The public has also learned to admire and respect killer whales by seeing them up close. But some people feel that such big and intelligent animals should not be kept in captivity.

Killer whales resting in British Columbian waters.

Killer whales on the move.

There is still much we do not know about killer whales. Are there resident and transient pods everywhere they live? Which males father the calves in a pod? How far do killer whales wander? Scientists around the world are hoping to answer these and other questions. But no matter how much they find out, there will always be more to learn about these intelligent, beautiful animals.

INDEX

(Italicized numbers indicate photos.)

age of killer whales, 17, 18

birth, 16, 17
blowhole, 6, *7*
blubber, 8
breaching, *1, 4*
breathing, 5, 6
British Columbia, 21

calf, *8, 16, 17*
captive killer whales, 28
color of killer whales, 5

ears, 13
eyes, *12*

fins, *9,* 10, *10, 11, 14, 15, 18,* 20, *20*
flippers, *10*
flukes, *11*
food of killer whales, 21, 23

habitat of killer whales, 28

mammals, 5, 8
milk, 5, 16

orca, 20

play behavior, *25*
pods, 26, 31; resident, *22, 23–25, 24,* 26; transient, *21,* 26

relatives of killer whales, 5

saddle patch, *20*
size of killer whales, 14, 15, 16
sounds, 13, 26
spy hopping, *13*
swimming, 6, 11
teeth, *19*

weight of killer whales, 14, 15, 16

METRIC CONVERSION CHART

When you know:	Multiply by:	To get:
Inches	2.54	Centimeters
Feet	.305	Meters
Yards	.914	Meters
Miles	1.61	Kilometers
Pounds	.454	Kilograms

These conversion factors are not exact, but give measurements that are almost equal.